WHY TRUMP WON
The reasons behind the biggest upset in America's History

Foreword

I must admit that, like many others, I bought into the narrative about the elections in the United States. Hillary Clinton was going to win. Polls seemed to be delivering a clear message and "serious" media analysts as well. There seemed to be little doubt, and those who expressed skepticism were quickly silenced.

Unlike many others, however, on Tuesday, November 8, I quickly realized my mistake. By the time Florida's vote count went to 95% and Ohio to 80% the conclusion was clear, Donald Trump was going to be the next President of the United States. The betting markets had not reacted, nor did the survey aggregators, but the trend was evident.

Florida and Ohio were the beginning of a trend that was consistently repeated, giving an unprecedented and decisive advantage to the Republican candidate in white middle-class counties in the decisive states. So great that it would be impossible to reverse by demographic groups favorable to Clinton.

Then I did what common sense advised me. I took advantage of having understood the situation before the others and placed a bet on Trump. I then went into a trading tool and bet against the dollar, assuming that, as predicted by financial experts, the currency would collapse when the news was confirmed.

The first reactions were indeed as expected. The dollar fell sharply against other foreign currencies as time passed. Suddenly, however, the trend was reversed. Not only did it stop losing its value but it became stronger and stronger, to the point that I had to withdraw my money immediately in order to avoid losses. And that was where it became clearer than ever: Trump's triumph was not really a surprise. There was logic behind it and I was very interested to find out what it was. And so came the idea of this book.

Over the next few days I read as much news as possible, talked to as many people as possible, and researched all the statistics that crossed my path. Little by little I understood the reasons why the most powerful country in the world had chosen a man who, by the standards of traditional politics, was completely unelectable. My first conclusion was that these elections were not really governed by the standards of traditional politics. And from there came several more.

This is a small book, which is not intended to be an exhaustive account of the election. The idea is to help anyone who reads it, liberal or conservative, American or from the somewhere else in the world, of any social class and race, to understand both the reasons for Donald Trump's victory and for Hillary Clinton's defeat. Because those two things may look the same, but they are not. And, from there, to understand what is next for the country and for the world, because there is no doubt that the next four years will be as intense as the election itself.

As you will see in the next pages, the names of the chapters of the book are precisely those reasons and the last is the conclusion and the paths to follow. I hope you find them interesting, and invite you to join in the discussion on Twitter @whytrumpwonbook, where, in addition, I will post the sources used to write this book and many more, related to the subject and the future of America and the world. Also, if you wish, you can reach me by email at whytrumpwonbook@gmail.com

Chapter 1. The bad candidate was Hillary, not Trump

The prestigious magazine Foreign Affairs published, in its February 2016 edition, an article by its editor, Nathan J. Robinson, called " Unless the Democrats Run Sanders, a Trump Nomination Means a Trump Presidency ". With admirable clarity, Robinson predicted, eight months in advance, what would happen in the election with Hillary Clinton as the Democratic candidate.

I will reproduce this paragraph, which encompasses the serious handicap with which Clinton started, before even beginning her campaign against Trump.

"Even among Democratic party operatives, she's acknowledged as "awkward and uninspiring on the stump," carrying "Bill's baggage with none of Bill's warmth." New York magazine described her "failing to demonstrate the most elementary political skills, much less those learned at Toastmasters or Dale Carnegie." Last year the White House

was panicking at her levels of electoral incompetence, her questionable decision-making, and her inclination for taking sleazy shortcuts… in a race against Trump, Hillary will be handicapped not only by her feeble campaigning skills, but the fact that she will have a sour national mood, a poor staff, and a brilliant opponent".

On Election Day, Clinton's campaign seemed to have done everything well. She won all three debates; placed each one of Trump's scandals under the spotlight; was at an advantage in the polls; had raised a lot more funds than her rival; and possessed the better "ground game". And yet, she lost, and she lost because the disadvantage with which she started at the beginning was too large, not because of what she did or could have done but because of who she was.

As never before, traditional politics are in a serious crisis. The image of the selfish, corrupt politician interested only in enriching himself no matter what happens to those who voted for him is prevalent both in the United States and in the rest of the world.

It's no coincidence that the reputation of the American Congress is at the lowest point in its history (13% popularity in the aggregate on Pollster.com), nor that the satisfaction of the American people with the way the country is going doesn't even reach 30% of favorability (28.5% in the Pollster aggregate). For the majority of the population, politicians are those who make political decisions, and if they are the wrong ones, there are no more culprits to be found.

Why then does Barack Obama have a popularity of 54%, after eight years in power? Because, as Bob Davis and John W. Miller mention in their excellent article "The Places That Made Donald Trump President", many people saw Barack Obama as the most suitable candidate to shake up the White House, And despite not having fully achieved it in the end, he seems to have tried his best. No one could consider Barack Obama and Donald Trump even remotely similar but something they had - and have - in common is that image of outsiders, far removed from traditional politicians.

As for Hillary, there is probably no more traditional politician across the United States. She would have been the second president in her own family, has held public positions for the past three decades, dresses in designer clothes, speaks always with political correctness and nothing she says seems to be subject to improvisation. And, unlike Trump, her vices were clearly the vices of a politician.

This is well described by Stephanie Coontz in her CNN article, "Why the White Working Class Ditched Clinton."

"Clinton kept things quiet, including the cozy and well-paid meetings that financial interests arranged for her. She and her husband financed daughter Chelsea's $3 million dollar wedding, and it's doubtful Chelsea would have landed a $600,000 a year job her first year after leaving school without those parental connections… They made their considerable fortune from profitable book deals and wildly-lucrative

speaking engagements. They didn't need to stiff anyone. But neither did their activities generate many jobs".

Another analyst, Helaine Olen, was even more blunt in her Slate article "Clinton Lost the Economic Argument".

"In an election in which there was clear rage against the meritocratic machine, Clinton spent August hobnobbing with Wall Street bankers in the Hamptons just weeks before (accurately if impoliticly) calling half of her opponents' supporters "a basket of deplorables" at a fundraiser that some donors paid $50,000 to attend".

Hillary didn't even understand that she had to distance herself from the traditional politicians from a graphic perspective. In an excellent analysis in the newspaper La Vanguardia, the Spanish creative director Javier Inglés, explained the huge differences between the campaign images of the two candidates and why Trump's were far superior.

"From an advertising or propaganda point of view, Trump is a person who has always presented himself to the world as a hard man ... The images of Trump's campaign apparatus showed that hardness and firmness that has always characterized him. In that sense there's no mistake with him. It's pretty evident who he is.

Hillary's propagandistic apparatus tried to create a world around her that helped her not to go through rough topics, trying to create a maternal and feminine image that in the end, perhaps, may have been one of the factors that have made her lose. It's easier to convey coherence, transparency, whether people like it or not, than a pre-designed or prefabricated message.

From a communication point of view she has made the strategic mistake of covering up a series of things about her past that she could have fought face to face and come out

victorious"

In the months leading up to November 8 there seemed to be a consensus in the liberal press that said that the only reason why, after eight years in power, the Democrats had a chance to win the election was because Trump was a lousy candidate. In fact, what they should have said is that the most important reason the Democrats could have lost the election was because Hillary was a lousy candidate.

Clinton could have had a good shot at any normal election against a normal opponent, but the process in 2016 was not normal at all and Trump was a very unconventional opponent. The most incredible thing is that the Democrats had a great opportunity to realize how different the scenario was in their own Primary and failed to seize it.

Let's be frank, if anybody had been asked whether a 74-year-old Jewish, self-styled socialist could become the President of the United States of America, the answer would almost certainly have been no. But that was what was about to happen with Bernie Sanders. Just as Trump did on the Republican side, Sanders understood that this election was going to be played under different rules and that the winner had to understand them. It was no longer enough to dictate policies from an ivory tower in Congress, or give speeches about which policies should be proposed, not without taking into account what was happening to a good part of the electorate. The problem for the senator from Vermont is that the Democratic machine had already decided long before that the candidate should be Clinton, and the best example of that are the emails that show how the Democratic National Committee favored Hillary over Sanders during the Primary that forced party chairwoman Debbie Wasserman to resign when they were leaked to the press.

Sanders, however, was far more successful than anyone might have been anticipated, to the extent that his bitter resistance in the Primary was often taken as a nuisance rather than as an opportunity to understand the electorate. And the Democrats paid dearly for their mistake. The 74-year-old socialist Jew had 43.1 percent of the popular vote and won in several of the regions with the largest white middle class population, including the states of New Hampshire and Michigan and some rural countries in battleground states, including the Panhandle in Florida, which, as we now know would later become critical in the general election.

Democratic Primary Results by County
(Clinton, Yellow, Sanders, Green)

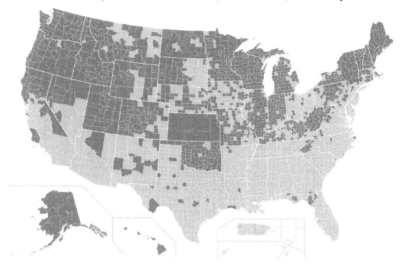

Source: Wikipedia

In his in Foreign Affairs article mentioned before, Nathan J.

Robinson went even further. This is what he wrote 8 months

before the general election took place, when it wasn't even

certain that Hillary would be the Democratic candidate.

"A Clinton match-up is highly likely to be an unmitigated

electoral disaster, whereas a Sanders candidacy stands a far better chance. Every one of Clinton's (considerable) weaknesses plays to every one of Trump's strengths, whereas every one of Trump's (few) weaknesses plays to every one of Sanders's strengths. From a purely pragmatic standpoint, running Clinton against Trump is a disastrous, suicidal proposition".

And it was. Clinton exposed Trump's behavior, denounced his scandals, got his victims to speak… And none of that mattered. And it didn't matter because neither Hillary nor the Democratic Party understood what those who ended up voting for Trump wanted. Sanders knew, and by the end of the Democratic primary, the polls placed him 11 points above the Republican candidate.

But Sanders was not nominated, Clinton was. And we all know what happened. Now, even some of those who voted for Trump are willing to admit that, with another candidate, the story could have been different. These are two testimonies collected by Stefanie Coontz in her article on CNN.

"The first words I heard were from a white waitress, who later confirmed that she had never gone to college, with whom I had idly chatted over the past few days. 'Bernie would have beaten Trump in all those swing states, just like he beat Hillary in many of them', she announced. Later, a desk clerk mentioned that her uncle had voted for Bernie Sanders in the primaries but for Trump in the final election".

Given the conditions, Hillary was the wrong candidate, and neither she nor the Democratic Party did anything to correct it. Her message was never addressed to the population that could have made a difference in the swing states, as Coontz describes, in this sentence, with which I close this chapter.

"I listened to Hillary Clinton's speeches over the last few months, looking in vain for any sign that she grasped the mounting frustration that so many working people have felt over the past few decades. While Trump talked about "the working class," she carefully focused on "the middle class." She mentioned tuition breaks and family friendly work places far more often than she talked about investment in infrastructure and jobs".

Bill Clinton once said, "It's the economy, stupid!" Hillary should have listened.

Chapter 2: A large part of America's population felt neglected, and Trump realized it

In principle, Trump's pedigree is not too different from Hillary's. The son of an investment banker, he was born a millionaire, and he has stayed like this for the rest of his life working in Real Estate and benefiting from tax exemptions. He lives in a tower in downtown Manhattan and has rubbed shoulders with celebrities all his life. Before becoming a politician, his only contact with members of the working class was with the parents of Miss America contenders.

But Trump understood perfectly that, in the world of politics, image is everything and became the mouthpiece of a group of Americans who saw themselves as ignored and unprotected for many years: the white working class. As a good businessman, he gradually changed his speech to suit his potential market. He left behind the liberal values he had once championed (a couple of times he had even donated to Hillary

Clinton campaigns) and radicalized the issues that mattered most to his target audience: immigration, jobs, security.

Take, for example, his victory speech.

"We are going to fix our inner cities and rebuild our highways, bridges, tunnels, airports, schools, hospitals. We're going to rebuild our infrastructure, which will become, by the way, second to none. And we will put millions of our people to work as we rebuild it".

The strategy worked for him. As Election Day passed, the results left no doubt as to whom the white electors of the working class had chosen. Thanks to them, and their votes in the Panhandle, Trump won Florida. Michigan, Pennsylvania and Ohio, which Obama had taken in 2012, were won this time by the Republican candidate. New Hampshire, a Democratic bastion par excellence, was almost painted red. Trump's bet worked.

In their projections regarding those states, the Democrats clung to statistics. Unemployment had dropped significantly since 2012, the median income had increased, the economy had generally improved. They did not understand that the election was not going to be decided by the absolute numbers but by tendencies and perceptions.

In her article in Slate, Helaine Olen explains exactly what has happened with the white working class and why, despite the numbers, their perception is a clear deterioration in the expectations of the life they thought they would have.

"These voters see their economic fortunes in relative, not absolute, terms, with other groups as their measuring stick. Many Trump voters, even if they themselves are better off than average, aren't living in particularly prosperous regions of the country. They often inhabit areas scarred by de-industrialization, drug addiction, and foreclosure, or rural areas where the jobs are barely existent. Housing prices may be soaring in Silicon Valley, but the reality in the Rust Belt is

something else entirely. Less than 24 hours after the polls

closed, General Motors announced it would lay off 2,000

workers at factories in Ohio and Michigan.

Others are way behind where they thought they'd be at this

point in their lives. True, incomes for men who never

graduated from college improved significantly in 2015, but to

say that increase made up for the ground this cohort has lost

since the start of the Great Recession—never mind the

1970s—is to engage in vast understatement".

In the past, a white man could be relatively sure of having a

prosperous life. He could work in the automobile or energy

industries throughout his life, form a family, give his children

the tools they need to have a good future and retire in

dignity. The 21st century leaves no guarantee, and it's only

logical that those who grew up with the promise of a steady

future want a return to a more secure past.

They were also the staple upon which the American dream

revolved: the quarterback, the cheerleader, the family

man. Millions of white Americans formed the backbone of the world's greatest power. Today that's not necessarily true. Bankers live as kings, celebrities can be of any race and religion, sports stars are usually black or Latino. For most of its history, the United States was a country of white Protestant workers; the last few years have completely changed that trend.

We should not think that it is simply a question of race (although it obviously plays an important role). It is more about social resentment. Many of those outraged voters voted for Barack Obama in 2012. They did not care that he was black, what they wanted was a change, and they were willing to support anyone who offered it. In 2016, between Hillary Clinton and Donald Trump, the choice was simple: the traditional politician against the perceived renegade. Those voters did not care if Trump was a misogynist, or if he had mocked a disabled person, the bottom line was the fundamental speech, one in which they were not only part of the conversation topic but were the main focus. Their country was going to be returned to them and for them that meant "Let's Make America Great Again".

Bernie Sanders himself, in an op-ed written for the New York Times after the election, acknowledged the problems of that part of the American population.

"I am saddened, but not surprised, by the outcome. Millions of people who voted for Mr. Trump did so because they are sick and tired of the economic, political and media status quo.

Working families watch as politicians get campaign financial support from billionaires and corporate interests — and then ignore the needs of ordinary Americans. Over the last 30 years, too many Americans were sold out by their corporate bosses. They work longer hours for lower wages as they see decent paying jobs go to China, Mexico or some other low-wage country. They are tired of having chief executives make 300 times what they do, while 52 percent of all new income goes to the top 1 percent. Many of their once beautiful rural towns have depopulated, their downtown stores are shuttered, and their kids are leaving home because there are no jobs — all while corporations suck the wealth out of their communities and stuff them into offshore accounts".

Many Americans voted for Obama in 2008 and 2012 and this year they decided on Trump. Some districts even underwent radical changes, which were decisive for the Republican candidate's triumph.

In 2012, Obama won Ohio, Pennsylvania, Michigan, Wisconsin and Iowa. All of them in the Rust Belt and all of them with huge numbers of working class white voters. Those were the votes that decided the election.

The New York Times, in a story called "Ohioans, Tired of Status Quo, Flipped to Trump for Change" collected some testimonials, which I reproduce here, because I find them very revealing.

"Mr. Noble, a lifelong Democrat, broke with the tradition of his union, the International Brotherhood of Electrical Workers Local 540, and voted Republican. 'I voted for Trump, and I'm not ashamed of it. He's straightforward and honest. He's pragmatic. At least he's willing to try something different.

'His points really hit home for us', said Jacob Hawk, 23, an electrician from Minerva, Ohio, who voted for Mr. Obama in 2012. 'A huge portion of it was just bringing jobs back to Ohio'.

'We were amazed,' Mr. John McCall, 70, who voted for Mr. Trump, said as he ate lunch at Athens Restaurant in Canton. 'Once you got to the middle of Pennsylvania, it was Trump, Trump, Trump, Trump. But where were her signs? There was just a complete lack. It was the same in Ohio. When we got home, I told my wife that this election is a complete lock'".

In the end, maybe no one said it better than ultra-liberal movie director Michael Moore, in an interview with Fox News's Megyn Kelly.

"You have to accept that millions of people who voted for Barack Obama changed their minds this time. They're not racists. They twice voted for a man whose middle name is Hussein. That's the America we live in.

But if you put people through another eight years [where] there's no middle-class jobs, they're struggling to get by, the basic things like the price of a box of cereal doubles ... these are the things that are important to people because they're living from paycheck to paycheck".

Of course, the race question can't be ignored when analyzing Trump's victory. Ultimately, the Republican candidate led a campaign that turned largely to white supremacy. A Reuters poll in June 2016 found that Trump supporters in New York State were more likely to describe African Americans as "criminal," "unintelligent," "lazy," and "violent" than voters who backed some of his Republican rivals in the primaries or Democratic contender Hillary Clinton. Stephen Bannon, appointed senior consultant and chief strategist by Trump shortly after the election, sprang to fame after turning website Breitbart News into a space where all forms of racial intolerance fit in and he himself, on his Twitter account, has consistently made statements against minorities.

However, to reduce Trump's triumph to the racial issue is to not understand the situation in which it takes place. There is, of course, racial tension in America. Every day and almost everywhere, but it's a tension that goes far beyond the skin color and, in the case of these elections, was manifested in those who feel that their lives have been usurped by others, Blacks and Latinos, of course, but also bankers and politicians. It's the furious reaction of a sector of the population that feels cornered and looks for a way out into the future, gazing back at a long-lost past where, in their perception, everything worked better than now.

To end this chapter, I will quote Arlie Hoschshild, a sociologist and author of a book called Strangers in Their Own Land: Anger and Mourning on the American Right, who explained the situation to reporter German Lopez in an article in Vox.

"'As they see it, they are all in this line toward a hill with prosperity at the top. But over the past few years, globalization and income stagnation have caused the line to stop moving. And from their perspective, people — black and brown Americans, women — are now cutting in the line, because they're getting new (and more equal) opportunities through new anti-discrimination laws and policies like affirmative action'.

As a result, Hochschild told me that rural white Americans 'feel like a minority group. They feel like a disappearing group. Both minority and invisible'

One can pick the facts here — particularly since black and Latino Americans still trail white Americans in terms of wealth, income, and educational attainment. But this is how many white Americans feel, regardless of the facts".

Chapter 3: The liberal press never understood what was at stake in the election

In light of the final results in the popular vote, and the great advantage gained by Clinton in the states with the most liberal voters, one might think that the disastrous performance of the liberal press would not have ultimately affected the outcome of the election, but there couldn't be an analysis of the reasons for Trump's victory without understanding the terrible meltdown of the major left-wing media in the United States over the past few months.

It seems to me that there is no better phrase to start this chapter than that of millionaire Peter Thiel, who after the campaign became one of the most important men in the Trump transition team. *"The media is always taking Trump literally. It never takes him seriously, but it always takes him literally. His supporters take him seriously but not literally."*

The first big problem of the liberal media in the United States is that they never understood that Trump was not a conventional candidate and that, in order to stop him, they needed to move away from a conventional coverage. In principle, an ideal media must strive for objectivity and run away from bias, and it's under this principle that the most important outlets in the country have been structured but, in practice, in America in 2016, everyone knows that there are liberal and conservative media and that each tries to push their own agenda and their own candidates.

Fox News got it. Breitbart too. And they got it essentially because for them it matters more to reach their audience and get good ratings than journalistic principles. The New York Times, the Washington Post and the Huffington Post, to mention a few, want to do both at once, and in this case it was a monumental mistake.

Let's take this example. This is the front page of the New York Times on Saturday, October 29, when FBI director James

Comey sent a letter to Congress announcing that Hillary Clinton's emails investigation would be reopened.

And this is the cover of the same newspaper on Saturday, October 8, when the 2005 tape in which Donald Trump boasted of sexually harassing women was leaked, which at one moment seemed like the turning point of the campaign, an event that would finish with the Republican candidate's chances for good.

You will see the differences in coverage between the two when you turn the page. Anyone would have thought that a newspaper as liberal as the New York Times would have given the Trump story a lot more relevance than Clinton's, right? Well, think twice.

For some reason, the headline of the Clinton story was written in capital letters and occupied three lines; Trump's, on the other hand, was written in lowercase, in only two lines. But that is not all. Accompanying Hillary's story is a photo of her, and two subordinate stories, Trump's reaction and an FBI analysis. On the other hand, Trump's leaked tape story is complemented by a photo of Haiti, a story of the same subject and another one about how Hurricane Matthew did not hit Florida as expected.

What was the editorial criterion? In my experience of more than fifteen years in the media, the decision was twofold. First, on the day that Trump's tape was leaked, Hurricane Matthew occupied an important space in the news cycle, so the editors of the Times didn't want to leave it outside the newspaper front page; when Comey's letter was released there was nothing else on the agenda, so they were able to display all the coverage. Second, the New York Times' ideal of objectivity "forced" the newspaper to give equal opportunity to both candidates, and on many more occasions this aversion to show any bias led them to treat Trump with far less animosity than their liberal ideals should have presumed. In this case, it happened as Thiel said, they took Trump literally and published the story, but they did not take him seriously, and they did not give him the coverage or the angle the news deserved.

Fox News and Breitbart, on the other hand? For days and days and days and days, their main news stories were related to the Clinton emails' scandal. Name the genre, interviews, news stories, analysis and opinion. Everything was focused on helping Trump's candidacy. They were perhaps less ethical but much more effective for the media's ultimate goals.

Now let's look at the New York Times' cover of the day after Clinton's email investigation was reopened (Sunday, October 30).

Doubts About a Promised Bounty

By now, it was already known that this FBI investigation would hardly offer new evidence against Clinton, and Comey was under severe fire for writing the letter. It's only logical that those angles would make it to the front page of the most important liberal newspaper in America, right? Well, not really. What were the main news stories that day? Two stories that worked against the Democratic candidate and one that had absolutely no reason to be there. The first was on the Democrats' fears that the emails could play a role in the election results; the second on Hillary's loyalty towards her assistant Huma Abedin and the third, a lengthy report on Genetically Modified Foods which was actually showcased in a flashier way than the ones related to the Election.

In fact, in the story about Clinton and Abedin, there is a phrase that sums up extremely clearly the position that the liberal press had throughout the entire election process. *"Now, with Mrs. Clinton seemingly in the cusp of winning the White House…"* The liberal press thought the Democrat candidate had the election in her pocket. And therein lay the second fundamental error of their election coverage.

A few days before Election Day, a curious controversy arose between the two most important survey aggregator sites. Ryan Grim, HuffPolster's Washington Bureau Chief, wrote a lengthy article criticizing FiveThirtyEight's creator Nate Silver for "only" giving Hillary Clinton a 65% chance of winning the election, against HuffPolster's 98%. Grim accused Silver of modifying the surveys with other factors in order to create the illusion that the race was closer than it really was. The article had the following gem.

"I get why Silver wants to hedge. It's not easy to sit here and tell you that Clinton has a 98 percent chance of winning. Everything inside us screams out that life is too full of uncertainty, that being so sure is just a fantasy. But that's what the numbers say. What is the point of all the data entry, all the math, all the modeling, if when the moment of truth comes we throw our hands up and say, hey, anything can happen. If that's how we feel, let's scrap the entire political forecasting industry".

In the end, the previous paragraph was totally right, only in the completely opposite way to what he had meant. Life is full of uncertainty, and being 98% sure of anything is a fantasy. With the exception of the Los Angeles Times poll, which consistently put Trump ahead of Clinton, no one else interpreted it that way.

In fact, despite what was published in the press and social networks, the surveys were not really wrong, after the final count of votes, it turns out national surveys were right in the general numbers, and the vast majority of state results were within the margin of error. The problem was the interpretation of these surveys by the liberal press and even the survey aggregators themselves who, in their eagerness to think Hillary had the election in the bag, did not consider the enormous inherent uncertainty in interpreting the wishes of millions of people with samples in the range between 500 and 1000 individuals.

In his excellent article on the subject, Media Analyst Thomas Baekdal explains the situation in the best possible words.

"There is generally nothing wrong with the polls. It's the narrative that fails. It's the media's unwillingness to report a 16

*percent point variance in the data. We are so afraid of telling
people that we aren't sure about something that we instead
focus on a single data point so that we can say that Clinton
will get the specific number of… votes.*

*And as a result, we end up looking like idiots after every
election. Our narrative told people something that turned out
not to be true, even though the data was pretty good.*

*We need to stop this. We are shooting ourselves in the foot
here".*

By no means could it have been presumed that Clinton had a
98% chance of winning the election. And yet, that was the
narrative of the liberal press. "Clinton has it in the bag!" The
New York Times gave the Democrat candidate 86% chance of
winning. Even the Los Angeles Times, despite the results of
its own poll, believed Hillary would get more than 300 electoral
votes. Instead of trying to analyze what could happen, they
simply repeated what they wanted to happen, and if that is a

blunder for any journalist, it's much more so if we speak about a media with the reputation of the aforementioned.

In sum, when I mention that the liberal press had a disastrous participation in the election and was one of the reasons for Trump's triumph, I do so because they made three major mistakes.

In the first place, although they did not create Trump, their role was fundamental in his meteoric rise. Since starting his career as a Republican candidate, the media never had enough of publishing his aggressive quotes, his crazy anecdotes, the strange behavior of his supporters. The tycoon understood better than anyone else that the more radical he became, the more space in the press he would have, for a simple reason. Scandal is much more newsworthy. People like to read about unusual things. Insults generate clicks and rating, fights even more. A political speech is often extremely boring; Trump's, on the contrary, always had something to comment, almost always negative, but always fit to be news. And that helped to put him in the spotlight, as more people felt identified with the background of his message beyond his incendiary rhetoric.

Second, the liberal press decided that supposed objectivity and balance were more important than evaluating the content of what was happening between the two candidates.

Trump had so many scandals that each of them seemed less important than the previous one, and the media were incapable of denouncing them, as they should have. Ultimately, a racist insult, a discriminatory attitude or an allegation of sexual harassment, should have, individually, been more important in the liberal agenda that an FBI investigation that ultimately came to nothing. And even if they were not, if there was a time when the partisanship should have prevailed over journalistic ethics, this was it. In an election with so much at stake, with a Republican candidate who represented a great danger to liberal values, they had to condemn every speech, every attitude, every word.

But it didn't happen. While the conservative press remained united and in message, liberals never understood what their priorities should have been.

And nevertheless, when making forecasts, it never crossed their minds that their candidate could lose! What would an indecisive American, but with Democratic tendency think when she saw that Clinton had 98% chance of winning? "My vote is not needed, I better get back home straight from work because I am very tired."

In short, the liberal press took Trump literally, but did not take him seriously until it was too late and he had already won the election.

Chapter 4: it was possible to game the American system and Trump understood it

Of all the Western democracies, only the United States has an Electoral College. There are some differences between systems, but almost all the countries around the world elect their presidents by popular vote. Nowhere, in a choice between two political parties, a candidate may have more votes than another but end up being defeated in the final result (sometimes by a landslide, as in this case).

At the time I finished writing this book, the official count of votes had not yet been finalized, but it was already quite clear that Hillary Clinton would have at least 1.5% more than Donald Trump. The figures, in millions, until November 14, were 61,039,676 for the Democratic candidate against 60,371,193 for the Republican. According to estimates by David Wasserman, an editor of the Cook Political Report, there were still votes to be counted, most of them in New

York, California and Washington, which would give Clinton an even greater advantage.

The problem is that none of this matters at all. The Electoral College was established in 1787, just eleven years after American Independence. There are many theories about why the Founding Fathers decided on this system, ranging from the need to maintain a balance between large and small states, -which is the most accepted version- to its implementation by the pressure of the southern states because most of their inhabitants at the time were slaves, and slaves had no right to vote, leaving them in a position of disadvantage against the northern states, where slavery had been abolished. In a system of popular election they would have lost every time. -Yale Professor Akhil Reed Amar, one of the most respected constitutionalists of the country, is the main advocate of this theory-.

Anyway, it's an obsolete and probably unfair method, but it's the current one, and political parties have agreed to abide by it in every election for the last 229 years.

Donald Trump has spent his entire life taking advantage of the system. As he said, he has found ways not to pay taxes many times throughout his life, he managed to stay afloat despite filing for bankruptcy at least twice, has been sued countless times but survived and has maintained a successful reputation despite much abuse and many failures in his companies.

Hillary Clinton, meanwhile, rather than take advantage of the system, she is the system herself. She knows the rules and makes the most of them. Together with her husband Bill, they have earned millions of dollars in talks and lectures, they have been very close to lobbyists and Wall Street and they have taken advantage of their many contacts. The Democratic candidate tiptoed all her life on the dotted lines but never really crossed them while Trump became an expert in doing so.

So if anyone could take advantage of the Electoral College system, it was the Republican candidate. Trump realized that what he needed was 279 votes to win the election, that the place to do it was the Rust Belt and that his target audience should be the white working class.

As I have said several times in this book, Donald Trump has absolutely nothing in common with his electorate. Born into wealth, he lived in wealth and will die in wealth. I doubt that he has ever done any manual labor in his life. Ideologically, he was always closer to the elites of California or New York (although he was never really accepted by them), than to the workers of the Rust Belt or the Panhandle. And yet, he understood that those were the votes that he should attract.

The math was easy. He had to take the states that Barack Obama had narrowly won and that were more similar to each other. The 2012 Democratic candidate had won Pennsylvania by 5.39%, Iowa by 5.81%, Michigan by 9.50%, Ohio by 2.98%, New Hampshire by 5.58%, Colorado by 5.37% and Wisconsin by 6.94%. The margins might seem wide, but not when compared with the 28.81% with which Obama won New York, Washington's 14.87% and California's 23.12%, not to mention the 83.3% with which he won DC!

Trump knew that with the exception of the rural areas of Florida he had absolutely no shot on the coastline states. So he prepared a speech that would appeal to the population of the states where he did have a chance to win, and radicalized his political figure to have the most exposure possible and reach as many voters as he could.

By this I do not mean that Trump did not share much of what he said in his campaign, but we have to remember that, before becoming a politician, his values were quite different. In an article in the Washington Post on July 9, 2015, Hunter Schwarz details the dramatic changes to Donald Trump in recent years.

"He loved Hillary Clinton; now he thinks she's the worst. He was very much in favor of abortion rights before he opposed them. And he might be running as a Republican today, but he was once a registered Democrat who called for legalizing drugs, a massive one-time 14.25 percent tax on the wealthy and staying out of wars that didn't present a "direct threat" to

the U.S. In many ways, he's been to the left of Clinton and even Bernie Sanders on some issues".

In fact, it's really worth reading the full article. Quoting him in different interviews, Schwarz concludes that Trump has changed his values on the following topics:

- Abortion
- Arms
- Healthcare
- Hillary Clinton
- Taxes
- Drugs Legalization
- Party Affiliation (He was a registered Democrat in 2001)

As he has done all his life, Trump took advantage of the system and used it for his own benefit. And he could actually have done it by instinct, by habit, rather than by strategy. While Clinton was spending millions on data analysts and advertising campaigns, the Republican candidate found a voice and an audience. During his rallies, he was listening to what people wanted and adapted his speech. Just like the conservative media, he understood that the goal was more important than the values to attain it, and facts eventually proved him right.

The results are impressive. In Wisconsin, Trump improved by 20 percentage points in 32 counties or more on the results of Mitt Romney, the Republican candidate in 2012. In Michigan he improved Romney's results in 73 of 83 counties. In Pennsylvania he did it in 62 of 67 counties. In total, in these four states, Trump won 47 counties that Obama had won in 2012. And it wasn't because people who voted Democrat that year didn't turn out to vote this time. Trump's discourse, be it true or false, appealed to the inhabitants of those regions.

In his extraordinary article Trump and the Revolt of the Rust Belt, Michael McQuarrie explains how his campaign team understood the possibilities Trump had in the region, and how he exploited them without too much effort.

"The Rust Belt had been effectively ignored for decades, so there were plenty of votes to be had there. When Trump's former campaign manager Paul Manafort laid out a strategy that included Pennsylvania, most treated it with contempt. When commentators like Michael Moore and Thomas Frank pointed out that there was possibility for Trump in the Rust Belt they were mostly ignored or, even more improbably, accused of being apologists for racism and misogyny. But that is what Trump did, and he won. Moreover, he won with an amateurish campaign against a well-funded and politically sophisticated opponent simply because he planted his flag where others wouldn't".

It's not surprising then that even Trump opponents within his own party have realized that the candidate understood something that no other politician had ever seen. Paul Ryan, the Speaker of the House, with whom Trump has had many clashes, admitted it the day after the election in a press conference.

"Let me just say, Trump's victory is the most incredible political feat that I have seen in my lifetime... He heard a voice out in this country that no one else heard. He connected in ways with people that no one else did. He turned politics on its head. And now he will lead a unified Republican Party".

Actually, someone else saw had heard the same thing and that was Bernie Sanders, but the tycoon was much better prepared than the senator from Vermont to use it and his circumstances were much more favorable.

As we said before, the Republican Party suffered from a severe lack of leadership. Neither Jeb Bush, Marco Rubio nor Ted Cruz were remotely close to being unifying figures. Trump won a Primary which, at one point, had an excess of 14 candidates, and that served him to perfectly tune his message for the general election. Sanders, meanwhile, faced a rival who felt she had the historical right to be her party's candidate after her surprising loss to Barack Obama in 2008 and had the party establishment behind her.

If we add Trump's ability to understand the system and take advantage of it, and compare it with Sanders' unblemished record, we can realize why the Republican managed to reach the White House while the Democrat had to watch the election on his TV set in Vermont.

Chapter 5: The challenge of Trump, America and the rest of the world

We have already analyzed the reasons for Donald Trump's victory. The logical question now is how will his presidency be? At this point, it's impossible to know. As a candidate, he promised so much and the promises were so different one from the other that it will be practically impossible for him to fulfill them all. Thus, this chapter will simply outline some scenarios, based on what we have discussed in the rest of the book.

Before we begin, it is worth analyzing the country the new president has received. America is deeply divided. Trump's strategy to become president was very effective but it further opened the gap between the different layers that form the society of the country.

In the days after the election, Twitter and Facebook were filled with news of verbal and physical abuse by supporters of Trump to people from different minority groups. At the same time, mass demonstrations against him were staged in New York and Los Angeles, in which hundreds of thousands of people participated. At the time I finished writing this book, 3.5 million people had signed a petition championed by Lady Gaga in Change.org asking the Electoral College to elect Clinton rather than Trump.

And then there are, of course, the popular vote results. With the rules that govern the rest of the world, Hillary Clinton would have been president. The country is effectively divided 50-50, and the division is clearly marked between whites and minorities, rural and city dwellers and between those with college education and those who didn't have it. America is split in two, and these elections served to give numerical support to a situation that has been breeding for years.

With this environment as a backdrop, there are several paths President Trump can take, and some of them have begun to insinuate in the early days after the election.

In his first speech as the winner, the President-elect seemed to have softened the aggressive tone that he showed during the campaign.

"Now it's time for America to bind the wounds of division; we have to get together. To all Republicans and Democrats and independents across this nation, I say it is time for us to come together as one united people. It's time. I pledge to every citizen of our land that I will be president for all Americans, and this is so important to me. For those who have chosen not to support me in the past, of which there were a few people… I'm reaching out to you for your guidance and your help so that we can work together and unify our great country".

A few days later, Trump gave an interview on 60 Minutes, and he generally kept the conciliatory tone. He announced that the wall with Mexico could be partially a fence, called to halt the attacks against minorities, said he would not seek to reverse gay marriage and had good words for both Clinton and Barack Obama.

But at the same time, those who have joined his transition team so far are the same ones who had major roles during the campaign, like Newt Gingrich, Ben Carson, Kris Kobach and Rudy Giuliani, along with his kids and his son in law Jared Kushner. Those are names that don't arouse any enthusiasm among opponents of his government. More worrying still was the confirmation of Breitbart News' Steve Bannon as a strategic advisor to the president. His extreme positions will make cooperation between the two parties more difficult.

The best possible scenario is precisely the one that Donald Trump highlighted in his speech, to be the president of all Americans. That he understands many of his campaign promises are impossible to fulfill and that he manages to seize the enormous opportunity of being an outsider in the political system. That he reins in his aggressive and irascible personality and opens his eyes to the needs of different sectors of the population as he did to those who ended up handing him the presidency.

Of course, that won't be easy. At this point, it's difficult to know who Donald Trump truly is. Where the person ends and the character begin. Has he become the tolerant man he foreshadowed in his first words as president-elect or does he remain the one who proposed a ban on Muslims and asked gun lovers to shoot down Hillary Clinton? Will he react violently at the first provocation? Will he push the nuclear button when Russia and China refuse to comply with his orders? Will he deport millions of illegal immigrants with the smallest excuse, even if it's counterproductive to the American economy? It's impossible to forecast any of that with certainty, but nothing is beyond the realm of impossible at the moment.

A Washington Post poll, published some days after the election found that just 3 in 10 Americans — 29 percent — believe Trump has a mandate to carry out the agenda he presented during the campaign, while 59 percent say he should compromise with Democrats when they strongly disagree with the specifics of his policy proposals. While this could be a promising sign, Trump will have to be tactful as those who voted for him are not going to stay quiet if he starts to renege on his core campaign promises. For them, Trump represented something completely different from a traditional politician, and to see him act as one would represent a huge disappointment. For a country that appears on the verge of racial and class violence, that could be a very dangerous cocktail.

Therefore, liberals should harbor no illusions. Trump may have softened a bit but in the end his government will be an extremely conservative one, and the tone of his campaign will never completely abandon his decisions. America will change a lot in the next four years and will definitely move to the right. It's difficult to know how much, but Democrats should be prepared for the worst possible scenario.

And, for Trump, there will always be the danger of a "Republican coup". It is no secret that the candidate was rejected by huge sectors of his own party. Because of his attitudes and turbulent past, of course, but also because of some of his political convictions, like his tolerance to gay marriage and his lack of religious beliefs.

There is no doubt that traditional Republicans would prefer the president to be Mike Pence, and Trump could well have the enemy at home. Pence is already the director of his transition team and another mainstream Republican, Rience Priebus, will be the new White House Chief of Staff. It wouldn't be surprising to see some people with whom Trump fought during the campaign end up appearing in his cabinet. The Republican Party would like nothing more than to "hijack" the presidency and make it go along the party's more traditional lines. Undoubtedly, there will be attempts, taking into account also that more traditional Republicans will dominate the Senate and House of Representatives. It remains to be seen if they will succeed and to what extent.

Another aspect to consider is the social fabric that remains after the election. America is a country full of resentment, and a radical presidency could exacerbate those tensions. We have already seen it in the actions of some whites against minorities in the days after the election and also in the huge anti-Trump demonstrations that have taken place in some cities. Although they are very unlikely to prosper, there are several initiatives in California to organize a referendum for the state to become an independent country. America is in turmoil and the policies of the new president could have serious consequences.

Also it remains to be seen what the Trump triumph represents for the rest of the world. It is no secret that Russian President Vladimir Putin played a key role in the Republican candidate's victory. Now that he achieved his goal, the relations between the two countries could have a major impact in the geopolitical situation of the planet. If they are kept in a positive trend, Russia's influence in Eastern Europe could very significantly increase, to the point that an invasion of countries like Ukraine and Estonia should not be ruled out. If, on the contrary, Trump responds to the usual interests of the Republican Party, his friendship with Putin will not last long and tensions between the two great powers will return.

At the same time, the new president has a decision to make regarding NATO, the military coalition of Western countries. As a candidate, he criticized the economic contribution of European countries to the treaty on several occasions and also threatened to leave it. Since his election, some presidents of the member countries have urged him to continue the collaboration and the decision Trump makes will have enormous consequences.

And what represents perhaps the most important issue, the 45th President of the United States will have to decide the country's policy with respect to global warming. A few weeks before the election, the United States ratified the Treaty of Paris, which promises to limit the use of fossil fuels and replace them with more sustainable alternatives. During his campaign, Trump mentioned several times that, in his view, climate change was a hoax and then appointed Myron Ebell, a climate change denialist, to lead his transition team on energy matters, which doesn't bode well for America's cooperation in global environmental efforts.

In the regional area, the main focus will be to see how his relationship with Mexico turns out. During his campaign, the new president placed special emphasis on the expulsion of undocumented immigrants, building a wall on the border between the two countries and the elimination -or renegotiation of the North American Free Trade Agreement (NAFTA)-, which ties the two countries and Canada since 1994. According to Trump, all these changes would improve the conditions of American workers, and those promises were a fundamental reason why he won the presidency. In that sense, he can't sit back and relax, and a quick and strong decision would send a message to his voters that he really does take their interests into account.

Of course, no one ensures that these policies will have a positive effect, and to strain relations with its southern neighbor may not be a good decision, but that would buy Trump some time in his early years as president.

I must say that, from an analytical perspective, the world will enter a very interesting period. After years of traditional politicians, this will be the first time that a real populist assumes power in a Western democracy over the past 80 years, and not any democracy but the most important one in the world. The consequences could be dire, however, and the planet could be forever marked by them. Hopefully, President Trump will have the intelligence to prevent that. And hopefully, the desire to leave his name engraved in history will also allow him to do something good for the world.

What is clear is that Trump's victory sends a message for politics in general. It's time for politicians to stop defending the great interests and put the people's priorities first. Language must change, strategies as well. Hopefully, from this tumultuous moment in the history of mankind, a new generation of public figures who are more interested in defending others than themselves can emerge. If so, these four years with Donald Trump as president of the United States of America will have been worthwhile.